# THE SPOUSE IN THE HOUSE

# BOOKS BY RICHARD ARMOUR

BIOGRAPHY AND LITERARY CRITICISM

Barry Cornwall: A Biography of Bryan Waller Procter
The Literary Recollections of Barry Cornwall
Coleridge the Talker (with Raymond F. Howes)


PLAY

To These Dark Steps (with Brown Adams)


LIGHT VERSE

An Armoury of Light Verse
For Partly Proud Parents
Golf Bawls
Leading with My Left
Light Armour
The Medical Muse
Nights with Armour
Privates' Lives
Punctured Poems
The Spouse in the House
Yours for the Asking


PROSE HUMOR AND SATIRE

The Academic Bestiary
American Lit Relit
Armour's Almanac
The Classics Reclassified
A Diabolical Dictionary of Education
Drug Store Days
English Lit Relit
Going Around in Academic Circles

# THE SPOUSE
# IN THE HOUSE

## by Richard Armour
### illustrated by Henry Syverson

McGraw-Hill Book Company

New York  Toronto  St. Louis
Düsseldorf  Mexico  Panama

Book design by Marcy J. Katz.

123456789BPBP798765

Library of Congress Cataloging in Publication Data

Armour, Richard Willard, date
  The spouse in the house.
  Poems
  I.  Title.
PS3501.R55S6        811'.5'2        74-23727
ISBN 0-07-002270-4

Many of these verses originally appeared in *Family Weekly*, but
others were in *Family Circle, Family Health, Good
Housekeeping, Los Angeles Times, McCall's, Postgraduate
Medicine, Quote, Time of Your Life, Together,* and *The Wall
Street Journal.* I am grateful for permission to include these
verses, none of which has previously been published in book
form, in the present collection.

Dedicated to Mort Persky,
Editor of *Family Weekly*,
who had the good idea of
making "Armour's Armoury"
a regular feature.

# CONTENTS

# PREFACE

Since this collection of light verse is about the home and family, I thought of writing in the manner of Edgar A. Guest, one of the few modern American poets not influenced by Ezra Pound or T. S. Eliot.

I had in mind, of course, his famous and often misquoted line,

> It takes a heap o' livin' in a house t' make it home.

I thought of saying that it takes a heap o' lovin' or, since you always appreciate it more after you have been away, a heap o' leavin'. But I was fearful o' runnin' out o' apostrophes.

For the most part, I suppose, these verses are about me. Not about me in an egotistical or egocentric sense, but about me as a specimen of this imperfect human race. So if these verses are not humorous, I hope they are at least human. They are about a fairly human being—or if most human beings are more human than I am, then about an unfairly human being, though I do not mean to be unfair to other human beings.

What I am trying to say, and the English language still eludes me, is that this is a book about the Average Man (me) and the Average Woman (my wife) and the Average

Home (ours). I make light, which I think is better than making heavy, or making dark, of our frustrations, irritations, and occasional satisfactions.

Not only do I make light, I make light verse. If you happen to prefer prose, I am sorry. I am sorry not only that you prefer prose but that I went to all the unnecessary trouble of fabricating meters and rhymes. However light verse has one advantage over prose. It can and should be short. After a dozen or so lines, the reader is through with that one and can start another. There is always the chance that the next one may be better. "Brevity is the soul of wit," as everyone knows. But everyone may not know that this truism appears in Shakespeare's *Hamlet* and was uttered by Polonius, who is not known for either brevity or wit. In fact he is one of Shakespeare's more long-winded and short-witted characters.

But enough is enough, an expression that has always fascinated me, it is so terse and unequivocal. It is time for me to get out of the way and let you read these playful verses. Much involved, you will find, is the institution of marriage, an institution in which I have been confined for more than forty years. For some odd reason I like my cell mate and soul mate (i.e., my wife) better and better as time goes on, no matter what I write about her. Though no sportswoman, she is a Good Sport.

If anything about me and mine applies to you and yours or to any other human beings living or dead, that is precisely what I intended.

R. A.

# ESPOUSING A CAUSE

I like "spouse" (the word, I mean),
I've liked it all my life.
It's masculine and feminine—
For husband and for wife.

The plural, spouses, though, I think
Is really not so nice.
I wish that one alone were spouse
And two together spice.

# DOWN THE TUBE

I've seen my wife with anger burn
At something that I never learn:
The toothpaste tube I squeeze and bend
At top and middle, not the end.

She scolds me, pointing out my error,
Makes use of scorn and taunts and terror,
But I forget and go on squeezing
The toothpaste tube in ways displeasing.

In larger things we are convivial;
What causes trouble is the trivial.

# TOO NEAT?

A woman who is too neat a housekeeper may be trying to work off her psychological tensions.—*News item*


And here I had equated neatness
With pride and care and love and sweetness.
Yet all the time that mopping, dusting,
Was just to keep her id from busting.

Oh, heed this warning from my pen,
You all-in-place, well-cared-for men.
Your bed is made, your sink is tidy,
As neat on Sunday as on Friday.

And yet behind that Duz and Drano
There lurks a smoldering volcano. . . .
And as for me, I'll no more mutter
But take it easy midst the clutter.

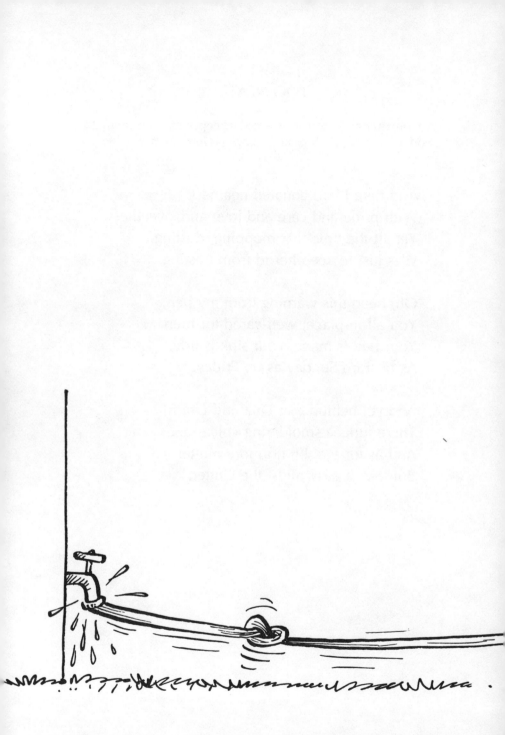

# THE KINK AND I

I have a garden hose that kinks,
And more than that, it feels and thinks.
This I conclude from much reviewing:
I'm sure it knows what it is doing.
If it could speak, you'd hear it boast:
"I kink when it annoys him most,
I kink when he is off his guard,
I kink when he's across the yard."
And when the flow becomes a trickle,
How it must please the hose, and tickle.
The hose has got what it was after,
And now it doubles up with laughter.

# SPOT CHECK

The window I wash,
The one with a spot,
Has the spot, I have found,
On the side where I'm not.

Leopards, I'm told,
Can't change spots on their hides,
But the spots on a window
Would seem to change sides.

For first I go out
And then I come in,
But the spot's where I'm not,
Just as certain as sin.

It must be my eyesight,
Not magic, I say,
But I mostly give up
And just let the spot stay.

## A MAN FOR ALL SEASONINGS

"Pass the salt," I say, and yet
Salt and pepper's what I get.
If "Pass the pepper" I should yell,
Salt would come along as well.
Like man and wife, like sister, brother,
Where the one is, there's the other.
Though salt has many times the takers,
Pepper's in as many shakers.
So don't object, and don't be loath—
Just ask for one, accept them both.

# ON THE MOVE

A woman requires but three things,
And life will but rarely bore her:
A table and chair
To move here and there
And a husband to move them for her.

# PURCHASE PRICE

In Turkey, where tradition requires that men buy their wives, especially in rural areas, the bride price in one year has jumped from $1,000 to $1,500.—*News item*

Such a sudden rise
In the going price
Should make a young Turk,
If he's smart, think twice.

Is she worth that much?
Have you shopped around?
Should you wait for a sale,
Maybe buy by the pound?

Is a trade-in accepted,
A pig, or a horse?
And what about sales tax
And extras, of course?

Better, maybe, buy land
Or a car or a boat
Or pay off your debts,
Whether mortgage or note.

When buying a wife,
This is only a start.
For the upkeep, you'll find,
Is the larger part.

14

# STEP RIGHT IN

We have a step that guests don't see,
Arriving in our yard.
They often trip, they sometimes fall,
They've come down pretty hard.

That step has caused some bruises, cuts,
And rather nasty sprains.
Some guests who didn't see that step
Are walking, now, with canes.

But, after years, it's being fixed,
That tricky little shelf.
What made me have it done at last?
Today I fell myself.

## TEAMWORK

A splendid team, my wife and I:
She washes dishes, and I dry.
I sometimes pass her back a dish
To give another cleansing swish.
She sometimes holds up to the light
A glass I haven't dried just right.
But mostly there is no complaint,
Or it is courteous and faint,
For I would never care to see
The washing job consigned to me,
And though the things I dry still drip,
She keeps me for companionship.

## SHADOW AND SUBSTANCE

Most women wear eye shadow.
I don't know why they do.
That bluish stuff
Must cost enough.
Takes time applying, too.

A lot more fun I'd think it,
At least with most adults,
To stay up late
And dissipate
And get the same results.

# PRETTY AS A PICTURE

I note, as I turn through our scrapbook,
To the end from the very beginning,
That all of us seem to be cheerful,
And mostly we're clowning and grinning.

Yes, everyone's friendly and happy,
Contented and nicely adjusted.
Not once does a face have a frown on
Or a look that is pained or disgusted.

We all seem to love one another,
There's never an ill-tempered lapse.
It's a scrapbook—and yet not a photo
To help us remember our scraps.

# ROOF TOPPED

We have, alas, a leaky roof.
It was, I think, the builder's goof,
Or possibly the architect's,
Or the inspector who inspects.
But anyhow, when rains descend
Our roof springs leaks from end to end.
We fill up buckets, fill up pans,
We try all sorts of schemes and plans,
But must await the end of rain.
No end, though, to the ugly stain,
The dampened clothing, clammy books,
The furniture with spotted looks.
Time after time our roof's been fixed,
But still the leaks have not been nixed.
I'm full of anguish, fear, and sorrow:
The forecast is for rain tomorrow.

# PICTURE ME

A picture hanging at an angle
Always sets my nerves a-jangle.
If it's awry a tiny bit,
It causes me to have a fit.

So at this moment, when I see
A picture crooked as can be,
Why don't I rise and set it straight?
What makes me sit and hesitate?

I'm not at home, I am a guest,
And I have learned that it's not best.
Some folks it gives a feel of guilt,
While others *like* a jaunty tilt.

There may be homes—alas, alack—
Where I'd not be invited back.

# WELL, BREAD

Bread stretches far in all directions,
Fills supermarket shelves and sections:
The whole grain and its chewy ilk,
Breads made with only non-fat milk,
The raisin, rye, and for the fickle
The stone-ground, too, and pumpernickel,
As well as sourdough, loved by Frenchmen,
With tasty crust for crusty henchmen.
Yes, bread with honey in its dough,
Bread baked by squaw or Eskimo. . . .
I stand perplexed, with dizzy head:
The note I carry just says "Bread."

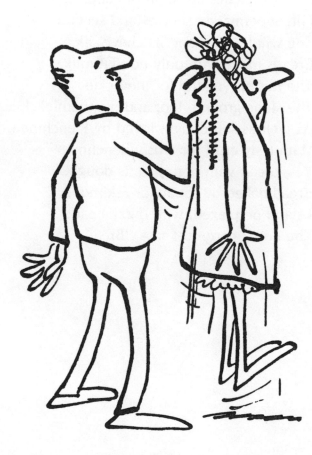

# BACK-UP MAN

My wife has a dress that I greatly prefer.
It isn't the one that looks best on her.
She has fancier dresses and far more expensive,
Her wardrobe's the kind that (I'd say) is extensive.
However this dress that I like so much
Has something extra, a special touch.
And what does it have? A zipper in back
That because of some feminine muscular lack
She cannot zip up, but must have some aid—
It's the way the dress in this style was made.
So she calls for me, with a plaintive yelp.
And I? Well, I'm always glad to help.
It makes me feel needed, a masculine man,
Which I think was the dress designer's plan.

# HANG IT ALL

Some are wood and some are wire.
I'll tell you what, if you inquire.
I mean the hangers hung in rows
Where, in the closet, hang my clothes.
Day after day, year after year,
At clothes and hangers both I peer,
And like a kind and thoughtful mother
I check the one against the other.
At times the empty hangers dangle
And oft with one another tangle.
A few too many, clogging, cloying,
Can be, I'm sure you know, annoying.
But that is nothing, *nothing* to
A closet where there are too few.

30

# BEDSIDE MANNERS

I lift no voice, I raise no banner
To praise my doctor's bedside manner.
It's not that it is bad at all,
It's just that he won't come on call.
But though I carry on and moan
He mostly just prescribes by phone.
And so, though he may be a whiz,
I don't know what his manner is.
His bedside manner, more or less,
Is very like my own, I guess.
That is, he yawns, turns off the light,
Lies down, and hopes to sleep all night.

## NOT-SO-GAY BLADE

My wife uses scissors for prying up lids with.
I use them for fixing the toys of our kids with.
We both use our scissors for dibbling round plants
    with,
For pruning our shrubs and for clobbering ants with,
For bashing a nail and for loosing a nut with,
And yet wonder why they're too dullish to cut with.

# MIXED NUTS

I hate the people who take the pecans
And almonds and leave me the peanuts,
Who take the Brazil nuts, the big nuts, the whole
    nuts,
And leave me the broken and wee nuts—
The people, in short, and I truly abhor them,
Who do what I'd do if I got there before them.

# CHAIN LETTER

Our bank has pens its patrons use;
On tables they are found.
The pens cannot be carried off,
For they with chains are bound.

Some, filling out deposit slips,
I note reveal disgust
To think that chains should bind these pens
And show such lack of trust.

But my reaction's different,
As I am glad to tell:
I'm glad the bank's like this and hope
My money's chained as well.

# SHOE STORY

I have some shoe trees made of wood
That I keep close about.
At night I put them in my shoes,
Replacing feet now out.

But I regret these trees don't grow,
As trees should, toward the skies
And bear a crop of splendid shoes,
Each one, when ripe, my size.

If such a tree I had, I'm sure
I'd tend it every day
And prop the laden branches up
And frighten birds away.

At harvest-time I'd pick my shoes
And, as I picked them, smile.
I'd hope that half were left, half right,
And all the latest style.

# STEALING AWAY

When we depart for, say, two days,
We risk a parting of the ways.
I say we ought to leave a light on;
My wife says no, and there's a fight on.

I say the burglars this will scare;
They'll think there's surely someone there.
My wife insists a light's a beacon
And burglars simply see to peek in.

Besides the glare and the publicity,
She notes the cost of electricity.
I say it doesn't cost a lot
To leave on just a 40-watt.

And so it goes, pro light and con,
To leave it off or leave it on.
Who wins, however, you must miss. . . .
A burglar may be reading this.

40

# HARK, HARK THE BARK

The bark of a dog gets me all upset.
I may lunge for the throat of some yapper yet.
And that's why it's good for my peace of mind
That the bark of a tree is the silent kind.
Were it otherwise, I just couldn't win,
Driven mad as I'd be by the constant din
And begging my neighbor with all my might
To keep his trees, please, in the house at night
And muzzled, as well, when he walks them around
Or they'll all wind up in the local pound.
But a lot like a tree, at times, is a dog:
There's no noise to his bark when he sleeps like a
     log.

# OH, HORRORS!

Horror movies don't much enlighten me.
They do, however, manage to frighten me.
They're full of happenings weird and miraculous
And ghosts and monsters and horrible Draculas.

The movie ended, I go to my beddy-bye,
Which I stand for a moment slightly unsteady by.
I'm only human, I'm not a Titan—
I go to sleep with my bedside light on.

## COMING CLEAN

I clean the junk from drawer and shelf,
From closet and from rack,
And look it over, I declare,
With thoughtfulness and greatest care
Before I put it back.

# WHAT WEIGHT PROBLEM?

Overweight people are less likely to commit suicide or suffer severe mental disease than thin people or those of average weight.—*News item*

It's really not so bad, at that,
To have a little extra fat.
The person who is overweight
Might just as well accept his fate.

Without that fat, he might live longer,
Be somewhat healthier and stronger,
But then again his nerves might jangle
And be on edge and in a tangle.

And so he lives a tranquil life,
Unworried by his work or wife.
He may be fat from feet to face,
But still he's not a mental case.

# COLLECTOR'S ITEM

A knock on the door
I'm always expecting.
I know what it is:
It's someone collecting.

Collecting for this,
Collecting for that,
And standing, the while,
On my Welcome mat.

Will I give them ten dollars?
A dollar? Two bits?
I stand there, uneasy,
Collecting my wits.

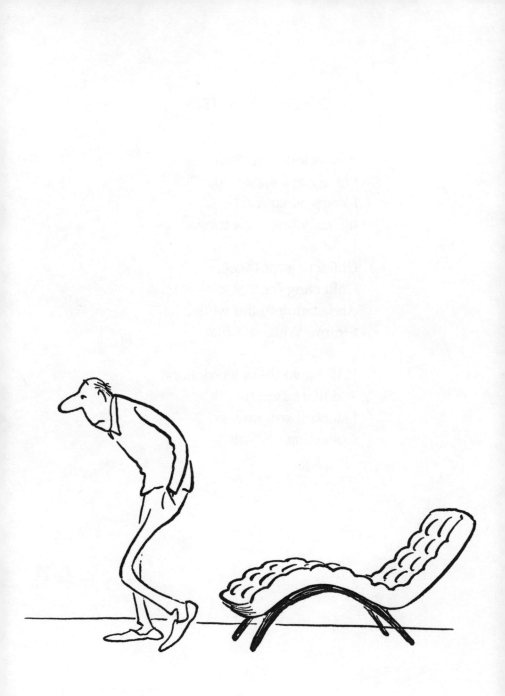

# HAVING A FIT

A contour chair I like to sit in,
For it's a chair I nicely fit in.
Indeed, although its shape is odd,
I'm like a pea that's in a pod.
I'm like a babe within its cradle,
I'm like the gravy in a ladle.
I'm like a hand that's in a glove,
A feeling that I dearly love.
I fit, in fact, so very well,
I'm like a nut inside a shell
Or like the coffee in a cup.
The only trouble's getting up.

# FAST CLIP

My wife clips recipes and ads,
Bridge hands and horoscopes.
The morning paper's full of holes,
The clips fill envelopes.
If I would know the daily news,
While through the paper zipping,
I'd have to guess what's on the back
Of every single clipping.

# SHOOK UP

A handshake is the oddest thing.
It's best when you don't wear a ring.
For some can make a setting buckle
And bring the blood and crush a knuckle.

Then there are those who, strong or weak,
When they have shaken, while they speak,
Hold on (and on) and won't let go.
You think together you may grow.

Between the two, I'll take the crusher
And not the holder-on, the gusher.
For if it must indeed be one,
Let fingers crack—at least we're done.

## GOOD OLD DAYS

Adam and Eve in Eden
Were fortunate, I declare,
Not wondering, "When is the party?"
And "What do you think we should wear?"

# ANYBODY HOME?

"Make yourself at home," I'm urged
By hosts when I'm a guest,
But I am very careful not
To do as they suggest.

For if I did, I'd take off coat
And tie and also shoes,
And put my feet up on a chair
And take a little snooze.

And then I'd turn the TV on
To something they'd find hateful. . . .
No, I won't make myself at home—
For which they should be grateful.

# HANG UP

Statistics show that most people hang up after three rings if the phone is not answered.—*News item*

If you're the phoner, it would seem
Three rings are surely ample,
And that is what statistics show,
At least this latest sample.

If you're the phoned, however, three
Are really not enough.
It makes the run from out of doors,
Or from the shower, tough.

As one who's oftener the phoned
Than phoner, I'd like more.
Instead of three, a paltry few,
I'd like much better four.

And better still, five rings or six
Or seven, even eight,
Although the chances are that still
I'd get there one ring late.

# RAG TIME

My wife's an incessant collector of rags.
With rags she fills boxes and barrels and bags.
What one day is clothing, all manner and sorts—
My shirts and pajamas, my socks and my shorts—
The next day's a rag. This distinction is subtle.
It's useless to argue or offer rebuttal.
When my wife has that look in her eyes, she's a
    fright.
I hide things away, and I button up tight.

## SHORT CHANGED

Bathtubs are made for midgets, I've guessed,
Or anyhow undersized runts.
I can get under water my knees or my chest
But never them both at once.

# FUN AND GAMES

With skillful hand and gleaming cart
I love to tour the supermart.
At Crackers I slip slyly by
A cart that's parked—don't ask me why.
At Macaroni, like a flash
I veer and miss a head-on crash.
Where Soup and Pickles intersect,
I'm hit and very nearly wrecked.
Near Frozen Foods, revenged, however,
I give that cart a swipe that's clever
And drive it nearly through a shelf,
Which makes me happy with myself. . . .
You take ice hockey, fights and all,
Take auto racing, basketball.
For fun and thrills, brute strength and wiles,
I'll take the supermarket's aisles.

# WIFE OF THE PARTY

At parties my wife
Is no talker, no wit,
Yet something she says
Makes with me a great hit.

When the hour becomes wee
And the small talk still smaller,
Except for the guests
Who their politics holler,

Come those words shrewd and timely
That bring me to life,
Words of wisdom and charm:
"Let's go home," says my wife.

# HOME REPAIR

We have a balky TV set,
As balky as I've ever met.
Repairmen come and go, but still
Our upset set looks wan and ill.
My wife, however, has of late
Come to the rescue. What a mate!
Now when the TV's out of whack
She gives the thing a bang, a smack,
And presto! Specks no more we view,
The lines are gone, the colors true.
I hit the set, it does no good,
But she knows how and where you should.
Just hard enough, but not too hard. . . .
She ought to have a union card.

# WAIT ON MY MIND

No argument and no debating,
What is, I ask you, worse than waiting?
I don't know anything forlorner
Than waiting, waiting on a corner
Or waiting by a ticking clock
Or waiting for a ring or knock
Or waiting for a card or letter
Or waiting payment by a debtor.

There's really nothing I hate more—
Unless it's being waited for
And knowing, hard though I may strain,
I just can't make it, can't explain,
While waiting at the other end
Is one who is (or was) a friend.

# WHO'S GOT THE BUTTON?

One day a button's slightly loose,
The next it's somewhat more so.
It loosens just a little bit
Each time I turn my torso.

It hangs, now, by a single thread.
It's perilous, let's face it.
This button is a special kind,
I doubt I could replace it.

I ought to pull it off, I guess.
My wife should sew it on.
I wear it slightly longer, though—
That is, until it's gone.

# PRETTY SHARP

Ninety percent of all facial nicks and cuts are made the first
time a new blade is used.—*News item*

Slowly though I plied my blade,
At least a dozen nicks were made.
Some cuts are really deep and cruel,
You'd think that I had fought a duel,
Yes, fought and lost, the way I bleed.
I am a frightful sight indeed.

And this I must admit is true:
The blade I used was shiny new,
Straight from its wrapping to my cheek,
And steel is strong and flesh is weak.
The second time won't be so bad,
But now I'm feeling I've been had.

Yet how avoid it? Pray, how skip
That first time to the chin and lip?
Here is a thought I've often mulled:
How start a blade out slightly dulled?
I have a way that's not the worst.
I tell my wife, "You use it first."

# MUSCLING IN

I've heard of what is often known,
And spoken of, as muscle tone.
What tone is that? I must say I
Have wondered whether low or high.
My muscle tone, upon my word,
I've listened for but never heard.
I've had a twinge but not a twang,
I've had a binge but not a bang.
My joints I've heard, their creak and crack—
I have a noisy neck and back.
My muscles, though, I can't deny it,
Must be high-toned, they are so quiet.

## INS AND OUTS

Here's a homely fact of life,
A truth there's little doubt of:
Baby's in his playpen, which
His toys, once in, are out of.

Each time you put his toys back in
He sends them whizzing past you.
It's mostly an endurance test,
And Baby will outlast you.

# CONSIDER THE PRUNE

Prunes are said to help the complexion.—*News item*

If this that we are told is truthful,
The way to keep your skin quite youthful
And without wrinkles, lines, and such
If you have lived too long (or much)
Is, publicly or on the quiet,
To see that prunes are in your diet.

And let me add, in this connection,
Another help to your complexion:
Just pick a prune up, closely hold it,
It matters not how young or old it,
And gaze upon it, note its state. . . .
Your skin, by contrast, will look great.

# TONGUE TWISTER

"He bit his tongue to keep from screaming"
I'm sure I've heard, or am I dreaming?
Perhaps I'm cowardly and weak,
Or maybe I'm some sort of freak,
But all my life, since I was young,
I've screamed when I have bit my tongue.

## CIRCUMSTANTIAL EVIDENCE

"I've just had a bath," said our son,
A wily and bath-dodging youth.
We were doubtful, a bit, of his words,
But the tub had the ring of truth.

# STIFF COMPETITION

I have a competitive neighbor,
A fellow who lives next door.
Whatever I do, he does better
Or faster or farther or more.

He says he does thirty push-ups,
While I do but twenty-nine.
He says he jogs two miles daily.
My mile and a half once seemed fine.

One way, only one, can I best him
And leave him chagrined and aghast,
And that's when I somehow maneuver
To tell him what *I* did last.

# PARTY LINES

I like a small party, just people I know;
To that kind of party I happily go.
The food and the drinks I can hope are the best,
But that isn't really the ultimate test.
What's important is having just four, eight, or six
And all in agreement on politics.
Still better (to this one I'll run and not walk),
Where everyone listens and lets me talk.

## FOOLED AGAIN

I must confess I look askance
At plastic flowers, plastic plants,
The ones that look so very real
That I must sidle up and feel.
It really doesn't seem quite right,
Infringing on the copyright
And making false so much like true.
If I were Nature, I would sue.

# RELATIVELY SPEAKING

I've relatives living near me,
I've others who live afar.
I've relatives I'm at peace with
And others with whom I war.

I've relatives who are wealthy
And some who are very poor.
There are those who are fairly decent
And others I can't endure.

Two kinds of relatives please me,
But few of either I've known:
The kind who leave me money
And the kind who leave me alone.

# HOME EXERCISE

Housewives are assured that doing dishes is good exercise for their arms and upper back; scrubbing the floor firms the arms, shoulders, stomach, and waistline, and dusting high shelves, if they stand on tiptoes, is good for the ankles, legs, and posture.—*News item*


The home is as good as a beauty salon
   For keeping a housewife in trim.
The rubbing and scrubbing and stretching and
     reaching
   Is great if she'd like to be slim.

No gym, it is said, does as well as a sink
   For strengthening shoulders and arms,
And standing on tiptoes to reach a top shelf
   Increases those feminine charms.

Just think of it, ladies, no membership fee,
   No lessons at all are required.
You know you have helped both your figure and
     health
   Each day when you start feeling tired.

Yes, housework does wonders for women, it's
     clear;
   Research finds it true, and don't doubt it.
And yet, though I've told all these facts to my wife,
   She isn't too happy about it.

# IT'S A GIFT

I sometimes (rarely) bring my wife
Some candy or some flowers.
Deciding what to get her takes
My best deciding powers.

It may be perfume, may be hose,
It may be cake delicious.
And is she grateful, is she pleased?
More likely she's suspicious.

# WHAT ABOUT MOTHER HUBBARD?

We've cupboard doors that open hard
And must be tugged and yanked.
Among our many nuisances
These very high are ranked.

We've also cupboard doors that will
Not close. They stay ajar.
Our banging on them doesn't help,
Or hasn't helped so far.

Oh yes, we've cupboard doors that close
And open, with authority.
I love such doors and so regret
That they're in the minority.

# COLLECTING MY WITS

My wife is a splendid accumulator,
In fact I believe there is no one who's greater.
Some collect stamps, whereas some collect pottery,
Some collect tickets for any old lottery.
Some collect photos to show they've been
    traveling.
Some collect paintings, some tapestries (raveling).
My wife collects everything—that includes
    wrappings,
Old letters and string and all manner of trappings.
With all she collects, our poor home is a clutter,
And I have been known on occasion to mutter.
But wait just a moment, that's not quite correct;
She's not a collector—no, things just collect.

# SUPER SPY

In supermarkets it requires
A super man or woman,
A person with the sharpest eyes,
Persistence, and acumen.

You see, it takes a special knack,
Sometimes, to find an item.
Signs are a help, but not enough,
And sometimes you can't sight 'em.

Yes, searching out just what is where
Is really quite a task,
And it is almost harder, friends,
To find someone to ask.

## OF ALL THE CHEEK

To kiss upon the cheek when greeting
I find is foolish, futile, fleeting.
It's just a brush, a passing blow,
A hasty bit of touch and go.

It must be even worse than this
For ladies, when the cheek they kiss
Is that of someone, Carl or Jay,
Who hasn't shaved since yesterday.

To kiss the cheek or ear or jaw
I would, I swear, forbid by law.
Upon the lips a kiss best lands.
It's lips for me—or just shake hands.

# NAME CALLING

I've heard about a stalemate.
It is a word, I guess,
That most, no doubt, have spoken
Who play the game of chess.

But I have come to wonder,
A thought I rather hate,
If stalemate isn't something
Referring to a mate.

Not mine, not mine, I hasten
To say—not such as she.
My mate is fresh as ever,
As fresh as she can be.

And if my mate I sometimes
Call fresh, she shouldn't wail.
She'd have more cause for worry
If I should say, "You're stale."

# FISH STORY

A survey shows that fish are the favorite pets.—*News item*

Some like cats and some like dogs,
Some go in for mice and frogs,
Some like parakeets and birds
Capable of saying words.
Some feed rabbits from a dish;
Most, however, favor fish.

Fish, you see, don't yowl or bark,
Never creep up in the dark,
Don't ask out and then ask in,
Don't shed fur from back and fin.
Fish don't beg for scraps of meat
At the table while you eat.

Fish don't sharpen claws on clothes,
Don't chew holes in garden hose,
Aren't tripped over, don't have fleas,
Don't run off or climb up trees.
Fish are favored? . . . Not to talk with,
Cuddle up with, play, or walk with.

# LEND ME YOUR EARS

I do not lend, I do not borrow,
For I have learned, much to my sorrow,
That what I lend I don't get back
Or if I do it's with a crack,
A dent, or something loose or rusted,
If it's, indeed, not wholly busted.

And what I borrow I forget
And might, in fact, have even yet
But that the owner drops a hint
(His eyes reveal a steely glint),
And if the hint I should ignore
He calls me up or bangs the door.

I do not borrow, do not lend.
It is a rule I do not bend.
That is, not often. When I do it,
I'll tell you this, my friends: I rue it.

## ON THE TRIP OF MY TONGUE

My wife I think is fond of me,
At times enthusiastic,
But not, as I can plainly see,
When I'm a bit sarcastic.

Sarcasm is a wicked thing
To have around the house.
It has a very special sting
When used by spouse on spouse.

My wife I shall subject no more
To sharp-tongued things I say,
Though I recall, alas, I swore
The same just yesterday.

# WOMAN OF NOTE

My wife is always leaving notes
To tell me where she's gone.
These notes are somewhat vague or terse,
And I feel put upon.

"Back ten," for instance, may not mean
At ten she'll home be lodged.
Perhaps it's an appointment then
To get her back massaged.

Today I found a puzzling note.
I'm frightened—do not scoff.
Just "Bridge" it said. Is that a game
Or what she's jumping off?

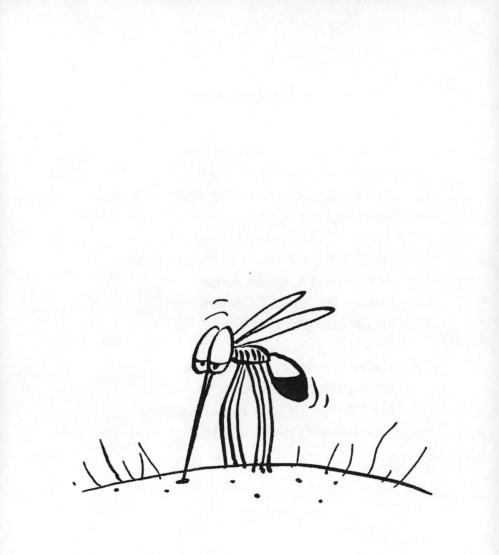

# INSECT ASIDE

Unsung and unhailed is the valiant mosquito,
Unflagging, unceasing, a charged-up magneto.
Though tiny indeed, with his little proboscis
He'll tackle grown men and he'll throw them for
    losses.

He spreads yellow fever as well as malaria,
And does it lightheartedly—no one is merrier.
He works day and night (more by night than by day)
And asks for no bonus or overtime pay.

People's blood in mosquitoes is truly quite ample.
Mosquitoes are always imbibing a sample.
But this is all wrong. What is needed, you see,
Is the blood of mosquitoes in laggards like me.

# HOME AND OFFICE

The biggest tyrants in the average office are those who are most henpecked at home.—*News item*

In the office he roars like a lion,
At home he's as meek as a mouse.
In the office his underlings quake,
At home he's henpecked by his spouse.

If the opposite's true, in the office
He's Milquetoast himself, can't say "No,"
While at home he's a tyrant and ruthless—
His wife has the bruises to show.

Each man, it appears, is two persons,
A regular Jekyll and Hyde.
No potion is needed to change him,
He takes the whole thing in his stride.

But what if a woman is working?
Does *she* lead a double life too?
And what if she works for her husband?
What's what, I would ask, and who's who?

I view such a situation
With more than a little concern
And hope that, however it's managed,
In fairness each one gets a turn.

# HOE, HUM

The man with the hoe
Is no symbol of labor.
As a matter of fact
He's my next-door neighbor.

And more to the point,
As I think you will see,
The hoe he is using
Belongs to me.

## MOTHER NATURE

My wife is on a health foods kick.
We drink our goat's milk raw.
Our whole wheat bread is whole, all right,
Ground by an Indian squaw.

We eat papayas, seeds and all,
And roots pulled from our garden.
Dessert consists of nuts and leaves
And raisins left to harden.

I'm fairly well, no worse from all
This food of which I've spoken. . . .
I must run to the dentist now
To fix a tooth I've broken.

# TRAPPED

I've tried to get away from it all,
But I've failed, for I've come to see
That though much, I find,
I can leave behind,
I can't get away from me.

# FACING IT

Our bathroom mirror has a bubble
That causes me no end of trouble.
I move my face the slightest bit—
The bubble makes a mess of it.
My nose is shifted to my cheek
Or else becomes a monstrous beak;
One eye (it's hard to think it's mine)
Is up or down and out of line;
My lips grow thick and then grow thin;
I look as if I've lost my chin.
That bubble shifts and longs and shorts me,
It unexpectedly distorts me. . . .
Bad as I look, at least I'm glad
I really don't look *quite* that bad.

# LEFTOVERS?

Leftovers are sometimes the things that we see,
Though the glance that we take is but fleeting.
They're items we know it is wasteful to waste
But day after day put off eating.

Then again they are things we would happily eat,
But where have they gone to? (One wonders.)
In view of the way they get tucked out of sight,
Perhaps they are really leftunders.

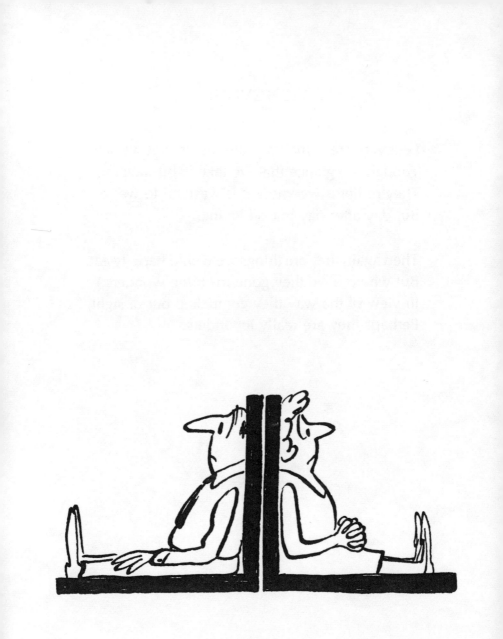

# BOOKED UP

There are many American homes in which there are no books.—*News item*

Imagine not a book around,
Except a cookbook maybe
Or phone book or perhaps a book
On "Bringing Up a Baby."

Without a book, what do they use
To keep a door from closing?
What do they nudge a person with
Who by TV is dozing?

What holds a pile of papers down
When there is windy weather?
What's used to press till glue is dry
Things being glued together?

Utilities are water, lights,
And gas? The way it looks
I'd say that there is more, much more
Utility in books.

# THERE'S THE RUB

One of my firmest disavowals
Is monograms on bathroom towels.
They may be good to help retrieve them
From guests who lug them off, don't leave them.
They may, although a little hammily,
Display an honest pride in family.
They may, to anyone who's curious,
Hint living that is quite luxurious.
And yet a fancy "B" or "W"
Can very often vex or trouble you
If when you'd like to dry your chin off
Its raised-up portion scrapes your skin off.

# NEVER ON WEDNESDAY

My wife and I can't both be gone,
Not Wednesday nights, at least,
For then a TV show is on
That I shall call "The Beast."

We've watched it, now, week after week,
With spellbound gaze we've looked,
And, such the plotter's shrewd technique,
I must confess we're hooked.

Each episode unended ends,
Suspense is at its height.
So ask us out to dinner, friends,
But not on Wednesday night.

# THINK OF IT

When I put on my thinking cap,
It really helps no more.
One day, I say, I need to go
Down to the clothing store.

I've put this off, because I fear
I'll shop there quite a while,
Yet buy no thinking cap because
I shall not like the style.

Still worse, the salesman in despair
May say, when I've tried all,
"I'm sorry, we don't have your size.
They just don't come that small."

# FAT CHANCE

Doctor Links Obesity with Desire for Love.—*Newspaper headline*

Love makes the world go round, it's said,
But here is something sounder:
A lack of love, we now are told,
Makes one unloved grow rounder.

Instead of reaching for a sweetheart
One reaches for a sweet.
An urge that nearly eats the heart out
Will make one eat and eat.

One snags a snack of this and that,
Eats more and more and more.
Hearts may be closed. What's open wide?
Refrigerator door.

Oh, let us all then love, be loved,
Be amorous and tender.
It is, to say the very least,
A way of keeping slender.

# DOG'S LIFE

Our dog is fed with bite-size bits.
When others stand, he calmly sits.
We open for him gates and doors
And ask not that he help with chores.
We let him sleep, hour after hour,
And do not wake him, do not glower.
We rub his back and, when he twitches,
We diligently scratch his itches.
Around our house, or anywhere,
I wish I got such loving care.

## PARTNERS IN CRIME

When a man marries someone much younger,
He's robbing the cradle, it's said.
But here is a little suggestion
I offer to people instead.

Consider the woman who's making
This man so much older her slave.
If he, thus, is robbing the cradle,
Isn't she, perhaps, robbing the grave?

# AND SO TOO BAD

I dearly love to read in bed
And while I read to munch on bread
With cheese or liverwurst or ham
Or peanut butter mixed with jam.

Yes, while I read, I sandwich in
Some sandwiches, and wipe my chin
If mayonnaise perchance should drip
Beyond my guarding lower lip.

Caught by a story, ere I stop
A bit of this or that I drop
And know by feel, or light of dawn,
Which side my bed is buttered on.

# MORNINGS AT SEVEN

My car and I have one thing in common,
And this I shall speak, if I can, with aplomb on.
Mornings, I've found, at an early hour
We don't have much purpose, we don't have much
    power.
My car's hard to start, but no harder than I.
My car wants to sit there, and I want to lie.
I haven't much get-up, my car has no go.
Quite small is our status, except maybe quo.
At least when the starter I press with my hand
And my car groans and sputters, I *do* understand.

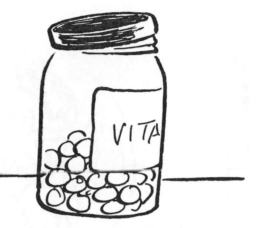

## CAN YOU TOP THIS?

My wife knows how to make me feel
As though I've muscles made of steel.
She has a clever little ploy
Which, though suspicious, I enjoy:
She hands me (big, strong me) whatever
She cannot get the top off. Never,
No, never have I failed or cursed.
(Of course, she gets it loosened first.)

# NECK TIED

I have a tie rack full of ties,
Narrow, wide, and every size,
Striped and plain and polka-dotted,
Silks and rayons, clean and spotted.

Yes, I have ties of every kind,
Ties subdued and ties that blind,
Ties that dazzle, ties that scare—
And the two I always wear.

# DO IT YOURSELF

Because of increasing costs, many householders are learning to do their own plumbing and carpentering.—*News item*

The hourly wage has risen so
   For carpenters and plumbers,
I too must try to learn a skill
   Before too many summers.

I'll buy a pipe wrench and a saw,
   A vise, and other tools.
I'll see about a course to take,
   Read catalogs of schools.

Someday—I hope it's very soon—
   Instead of wildly staring
When something maybe springs a leak,
   I'll do my own repairing.

And while I'm at it, since the fees
   Of doctors, too, are soaring,
In books of medicine you'll find
   That I'll be busy poring.

Ah yes, imagine please the scene,
   You'll not have long to wait:
I've just anesthetized myself,
   And now I'll operate.

# CAN DO

Our trash can quickly filled with trash.
We bought a second, feeling rash.
That trash can filled in just a wink.
Does trash, then, swell? Do trash cans shrink?

Although it seemed a bit absurd,
We did, in time, procure a third,
And that too filled up to the top
With trash each week. Where will it stop?

With trash I stuff each can, and rant:
The thing is not a can but can't.

## GET THIS STRAIGHT

Our teen-age daughter's teeth are straightened.
She finds it quite a thrill.
Her braces all are off at last,
And I'm braced for the bill.

Her teeth are in, my cash is out,
The job ran rather high.
Tight-lipped for months, now she can smile
More readily than I.

# THUMB TACTICS

I do not think I'm really dumb,
And yet the saying, "rule of thumb,"
I find is baffling, odd of meaning.
Toward this—then that—I find I'm leaning.

Is it a measure, say an inch?
(One's always with me, that's a cinch.)
Or since a thumb (my wife's) I'm under,
Is it that kind of rule, I wonder?

A thumb can make me smile or frown;
Thumbs up, that is, or else thumbs down.
Thumbs are for all the types, all ages,
Since some thumb rides and some thumb pages.

This "rule of thumb" makes me a fool;
I like my thumb, though, as a rule.

# TONIGHT'S THE NIGHT

Tonight I think I'll read a book.
At television I'll not look—
That is, until this program's through.
I wonder what's on Channel Two.
I mustn't miss that travelogue,
Instructions, too, on how to jog,
An interview—my eyes are red.
I'll catch the news, then go to bed,
Unless I watch those heavies fight. . . .
I'll read a book tomorrow night.

## WEEKEND WEAKENED

Late afternoon of Friday,
Or when that day departs,
Though things till now were tidy
The weekend syndrome starts.

The plumbing blows a gasket,
The lighting blows a fuse.
The TV's like a casket:
All dark—no shows, no news.

Through Saturday and Sunday
Our house is damp and drear.
It's just two days till Monday
But seems at least a year.

# GOLDEN TRASHERY

"He who steals my purse steals trash. . . ."
I'd call that statement rather rash,
At least applied to purse or wallet,
Whatever you prefer to call it,
Containing driver's license, which
When lost makes moods as black as pitch,
And credit cards affording surety,
And memberships, Social Security,
As well as snapshots irreplaceable
Of child or grandchild, hardly faceable.
Who steals my purse affects my life.
I'd just as soon they'd steal my wife
(Assuming, once I felt the lack,
They'd very kindly bring her back).

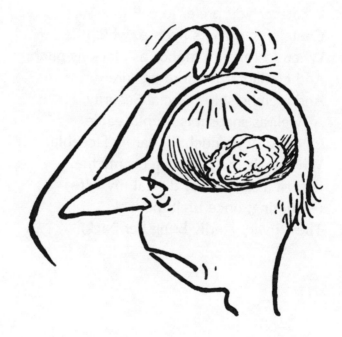

# ON THE BRAIN

The average human brain weighs a little over three pounds. The male brain weighs a few ounces more than the female brain. However the size of the brain seems to have no direct bearing upon intelligence.—*News item*

Until I reached those final words
I thought of bird-brains not in birds,
Brains short some ounces on the scales
And found most often not in males.

I was prepared to shout with glee
And gloat, as is the way with me,
And tell my wife what I had found
And walk two inches off the ground.

I thought of Shakespeare, Aristotle,
The makers of the flip-top bottle,
And other greats—all men, all wise—
Whose brains were surely super size.

And then I read that final sentence,
And now I'm going through repentance.
Whatever's wrong, dear, this is plain:
It's not the smallness of your brain.

# FULL HOUSE

Our house is full of bric-a-brac,
From top to bottom, front to back.
We've ashtrays, vases, whole or part,
And many so-called works of art
(Called art by some, our friends and brothers,
Called junk, I'm sad to say, by others).

We've things of china, things of brass,
And some of rusted iron, alas.
We've items of this year, this week,
And items thought to be antique.

If we should move, it is expected
We'd give or sell what we've collected.
We'll never move, though, far or nigh,
And all this bric-a-brac is why.

# VERBAL BURBLE

To "husband" means to save, be sparing,
Economize, for cash be caring.
It means to keep what you have got,
Be it a little or a lot.

That is, I guess, a husband's mission.
I rather like this definition.
It makes me, as I scrimp and save,
Think husbands all should thus behave.

But though I've searched the dictionary
And looked until my eyes are stary,
The verb to "wife" I did not meet
Except as "marry" (obsolete).

And I would never be so rash
As ask my wife, "Please wife this cash."

## IN THE SAME PLACES

I've seen my wife through thick and thin,
But don't mean cash or weather.
We started thin, long years ago—
Now we've grown thick together.

# THAT'S HOW THE COOK CRUMBLES

Consider how the housewife reads
A cookbook and its counsel heeds
And how she adds, with spoons and pinches,
Some cheese and chives, and never flinches,
Adds pepper also, pours in wine,
And tests it well and finds it fine,
Then serves her triumph, happy-faced,
To guests who salt before they taste.

# HOME REMEDY

Dogs have been prescribed as "home psychiatrists" for depressed people.—*News item*

You need not lie upon a couch
For this psychiatrist
And answer questions Freudians
Would probingly insist.

This "home psychiatrist" of course
Might lie down by your side
And, asking not a thing of you,
There calmingly abide.

Or else he might look up, warm-eyed,
And seem to understand,
And maybe paw your sleeve a bit
Or even lick your hand.

He might relax, relaxing you,
And go to sleep, lie still.
Of this, however, be quite sure:
He wouldn't send a bill.

# BIRTH PAINS

Stop it! Stop it! Must you sing
That silly "Happy Birthday" thing?
Must I have a birthday cake?
Must I grin a grin that's fake?
Must I blow the candles out?
Must I eat a piece, though stout?
Must I read aloud each note,
Some with rhymes that hurt my throat?
Must I, then, unwrap each gift,
Bought, I know, with canny thrift?

If I must, then tell me why.
Look me, meanwhile, in the eye.
When you've told me, tell me then
Why, like other grown-up men,
I must feel dejected, rotten,
When my birthday is forgotten.

# RIGHT DRESS

When my wife goes out shopping and looks for a
    dress,
I wish her, I tell her, the greatest success.
This means that I hope that she finally eyes
A dress the right color, a dress in her size;
Something slimming her hips, and well hiding her
    bulges;
A dress, though, that what is worth showing
    divulges.

But the one kind of dress that I'll urge her to keep
Is a dress that is pretty—I mean pretty cheap.

## FOR THE BIRDS

We have a bird bath in our yard,
And birds enjoy it greatly.
We thought it was a good idea
But we have wondered lately.

The birds have disappointed us,
So far have dashed our hope.
We cannot get them, yet, to use
The wash rag and the soap.

# SHELVED

In our bedroom and bathroom the shelves abound.
There would seem to be plenty to go around.
There are shelves for my wife, there are shelves for
    me;
There ought to be plenty, I think you'll agree.
But I gave up a shelf, like a diplomat,
For the stuff my wife uses to fight against fat,
And a shelf for some bottles she bought at a store
And now stores at home (I'm just glad there aren't
    more),
And a shelf for some articles left behind
By my mother-in-law, that we happened to find,
And a shelf and a shelf. . . . Now I've come to the
    edge,
With my toothbrush and paste on a window ledge.
Am I generous? Weak? Well, you cannot deny
That an utterly shelfless fellow am I.

# QUITE A DISH

A woman wasn't made to wash dishes. A dishwasher was
made to wash dishes.—*Advertisement*

I guess I must be quite a dunce,
For this I'd never thought of once.
Before I wed, among my wishes
Was someone who would wash the dishes
And also do such household chores
As make the beds and scrub the floors
And sew on buttons, mend my socks,
And dig around the hollyhocks.
Oh yes, and cook and clean the oven
And maybe do a little lovin'.

If we should have machines to do
The dishes and the cleaning too,
As well as sew and cook and mend
And flowers in the garden tend,
I'd somehow still prefer my wife,
With skills so very rich and rife,
Who takes no oiling, no repairing,
And also has a way of caring.
Dishwashing she may not be made for;
There's no machine, though, that I'd trade for.

# ADOLESCENCE

Adolescents adolesce.
It's something they must do, I guess.
To adolesce is to go through
A stage, as other creatures do.
The butterfly, that's oft a thriller,
Must be a while a caterpillar.

Now don't expect too much, my friends,
When one day adolescence ends.
There won't be such amazing things
As, for example, sprouting wings
Or other alterations strange.
It will, though, be a welcome change.

# TIME CAPSULE

This sums up married life,
No need for saying more:
A husband's waited on,
A wIfe is waited for.

# BY THE WEIGH

Our bathroom scales weigh two pounds light.
I check them closely every night.
My wife, too, knows the scales are thus,
But they're not rigged because of us.
I fix the scales with artful thumb
Just for the sake of guests who come
And who, soon after they arrive,
Ask "Mind if I?" and bathward dive.
No need to offer or to urge,
And afterward, when they emerge,
They're smiling, friendly, and, we've found,
Relaxed, and fun to have around.
Some from a distance drive, some walk,
Some come for bridge, some come to talk.
Some just drop in, or so they say.
We know they really come to weigh.

# ON THE RUN

Running in place is recommended for those who are unable to get outside to exercise.—*News item*

Running in place is a splendid thing
To do in your living or bedroom,
As long as the floor is quite sturdily built
And you're sure you have plenty of headroom.

No fear of a dog at your heels, and no fear
Of neighbors persistently gawking.
No need to slow down for a car or a bike,
Thus forced to leave running for walking.

Oh, running in place I know well, all too well;
It seems that my life has been such.
All these years I have run, like a fool run and run,
And never got anywhere much.

# HAPPY RETURNS

My neighbor's a very generous man—
I remain in his debt, try hard as I can.
His leaves drift over with every breeze
And fall in my yard from his shedding trees.

I can tell from his looks, I don't have to suppose,
When I swish them back with my garden hose
Or sweep them homeward where they were grown,
That he meant his leaves as a gift, not a loan.

## ON MY CONSCIENCE

My conscience is a small, weak thing,
Unhandsome, too. So be it.
I'm glad, unlike my nose and hair,
It's hidden deep within me where
My friends and foes can't see it.

# MIRROR, MIRROR, MIRROR

When shopping for clothes, I confess I'm a fearer
Of that fiendish reflector, the three-sided mirror.
My front, though not pleased with, at least I am
    used to,
Yes, rather relaxed with and sometimes amused,
    too.
However, the sight of the rear and the side of me,
The oddly constructed and somewhat too wide of
    me,
The view seen so seldom, less lovely than hately,
Is why I've not been to a clothing store lately.

## JOINING THE FOLD

Things that fold, like folding chairs
And folding tables, folding cases,
I lack the skill to figure out,
Or nerve, in public places.

Though others fold the things that fold
Upon the floor or shelf,
Before, impatient, I can fold
Such things—I fold, myself.

# NO DEFENSE AGAINST IT

Most women, anyhow the bulk,
Do something that is known as sulk,
Or much the same, I have no doubt,
They turn their lips down and they pout.
They say no word, they make no sound,
And this is part of it, I've found.
The "silent treatment" it is called
And leaves men helpless and appalled.
Men try to solace, try to flatter,
But nothing really seems to matter.
It's woman's way, it's not a crime,
And passes, happily, in time.

# OUT OF JOINT

One of the most frequent causes of domestic strife is the keeping of a joint bank account.—*News item*

Some little things cause bitter strife
Between a husband and a wife.
At one especially I'll point:
The bank account that's known as joint.

You know, it's really rather funny
The way two people can't mix money,
At least not if the two are married
And if financially they're harried.

As sure as there's but one account,
No matter, really, what amount,
There's tug and haul, there's constant friction,
There's quarreling and malediction.

Well, I who ask but peace, my friends,
Have found financial feuding ends
And everything is hearts and flowers
When money's parceled: Hers and Ours.

# TOYING WITH TOYS

Our children get toys from friends,
They get them from relatives too,
And many are toys that break—
We mend them with tape and glue.

Our children get toys for Christmas,
For birthdays, for any old time.
The generous givers are many,
And all I would thank in rhyme.

Our children get toys they scatter,
At finding odd places they're clever.
The givers of toys pick them *out,*
But we pick them *up,* however.

# NO SHOW

Though we have traveled quite a bit
And seen some scenes, we must admit
Apologies profuse we owe you:
We've not a slide that we can show you.
We have no camera, no tripod;
We bipeds barely have a bipod.
We have no meter that we treasure,
The waxing, waning light to measure.
Our pictures all are in our minds,
And these are hard to screen, one finds.
At least we shall not bore you, for
Our heads are what you'd have to bore
To see, arranged on mental shelves,
The pictures that we show ourselves.

# HOLD ON

You men who climb the ladder of success
And stand upon the top, all flushed and heady,
I hail you, but I also hail, no less,
Your wives, below, who hold the ladder steady.

## SHOOTING THE BREEZE

My wife prefers the windows down,
What air comes in is trifling.
I beg to have the windows up,
And cry that it is stifling.

She hates a draft, I like a breeze,
And, for your information,
When she is cross and I am cross
We get cross ventilation.

# COMPANY, ATTENTION

We've company coming for dinner,
Some people we've hopes of impressing.
My wife has her cookbooks all open—
She's trying a new salad dressing.

She's splurged on the finest of sirloin.
She seems to have lost all her reason.
The fancy dessert is a dilly,
With fruits that are long out of season.

She's working all day in the kitchen
And trying to get things just right. . . .
How I wish we could eat by our lonesome
The way we are eating tonight.

# WHO'S A HEAD?

*Father is no longer head of the family in America.—News item*

If Father's been deposed as head,
Who is it who is head instead?
If Father has been tumbled down,
Who is it now who wears the crown?

Could it be Mother, next in line,
Who has "The Queen" upon a sign
And rules the roost as well as roast
And is, without a doubt, the most?

Or is it Junior, almost grown,
Who runs the show, and makes it known?
Or could it possibly be Sis,
A rather subtle, coaxing miss?

With some it's one, with some another:
It's Father, Junior, Sis, or Mother.
With some (on this I'll not enlarge)
These days, I'd say, no one's in charge.

# TIME TYPES

Friends we have who are always on time.
Lateness they think is a horrible crime.
We set our clocks by the hour they appear,
And race to be ready so they'll not sneer.

If the doorbell rings on the very dot,
We know who it is and who it is not.
For we've also friends, I am quick to state,
Who are always—and I mean always—late.

The punctual people make us rush.
If we're not quite dressed, we stammer and blush.
The ones who are late, although good as gold,
Make our nerves grow tense and the food grow
    cold.

What of us? We're the kind who cause most
    enragement,
Forgetting entirely we had an engagement.

# NECK AND NECK

"You're a pain in the neck,"
My wife often would say
When I caused her annoyance
In some silly way.
With passage of years
That old pain is still there,
In the back of her neck
And just under her hair.
As a matter of fact
I've grown more of a wreck
And also admit
I've a pain in *my* neck.
But I don't cause my wife's
And she doesn't cause mine:
We both have arthritis
In joints of the spine.

# THE WORN TURNS

Be it a shirt, a pair of slacks,
A sweater, skirt, or blouse,
Once it is worn around the edge
It's worn around the house.

A paradox is this, I think,
Without the slightest doubt:
An article of clothing that's
Worn out is not worn out.

## RING MASTER

Women's earrings vary greatly.
I've seen some really odd ones lately.
Some look like rings for birds to cling on
Or circus acrobats to swing on,
While others look like buttons which
When pressed would maybe turn a switch.
Still others look like chandeliers
Suspended from high-ceilinged ears.

I've thought, "If only such an earring
Would help not only looks but hearing,
I'd take two from my good wife's shelf
And wear one on each ear myself."

## LOSING BATTLE

This, I have learned,
Is children's technique:
They whittle you down
Till you're helplessly weak,

Then even the smallest,
Most innocent tyke,
Instinctively knowing
The moment, will strike.

So here is the sequence—
No parent can win:
First you give out,
And then you give in.

# THE PEACEMAKER

My wife and I have arguments,
But they don't last for long.
In fact, they're over just as soon
As I admit I'm wrong.

# UPLIFTING REMARK

With today's emphasis on youth, face-lifting is becoming increasingly commonplace.—*News item*

We often wonder whether years
And he have made their peace,
Or maybe inner goodness foils
The wrinkle, sag, and crease.

Or then again, is all that look
Of smoothness and of youth
The work of surgeon's skill and knife,
To tell the simple truth?

To lift the face is done so much
We just assume it now,
And next we hope they'll learn to lift
Our spirits, too, somehow.

# THERE'S A CATCH TO IT

I cannot catch a ball that's thrown.
That kind of talent I don't own.
Be it a baseball, basket, foot,
My hands don't reach where it is put.
But I can catch a cold all right,
And keep it, too, both day and night.
You'd think a germ so very small
Would be much harder than a ball,
But no, without a glove or mitt
I'm very good at catching it.
If there were just a game I knew
Where catching germs of cold or flu
Would be applauded—this I know:
I'd be a star, I'd be a pro.

# FLESH POT

I've seen my wife put on her girdle,
A sight that makes my bloodstream curdle.
She tugs, she twists, she strains, she wiggles;
Absurd it is, but gets no giggles.
At last it's on—that is, she's in it.
So tight it fits, no need to pin it.
Her shape, there can be little doubt of it,
Is better when she's in than out of it.
And yet, beneath, although unwanted,
The bulgy flesh remains undaunted.
Yes, though it's squeezed and lowered, lifted,
It's all still there, it's merely shifted.

# PROTECTIVE CUSTODY

Grandparents have an advantage on parents—
Their lesser responsibility.
But parents come closer, their years being fewer,
To matching their children's agility.

Grandparent's are told, "You're in charge, he's all
     yours,"
Though maybe for only an hour,
But after ten minutes of watching and leaping
They question their staying power.

Oh, grandparents try to be ever alert,
Want parents with trust to receive them,
Then sigh with relief when there's Changing of
    Guards
And the parents return to relieve them.

# PURE SPECULATION

Though I can't tell, just at a glance,
There must be good mosquitoes, ants,
As well as flies and gnats and vermin.
It's something that I can't determine.

Such creatures, having lived good lives,
I wonder, when the day arrives
They shuffle off this mortal coil,
What's their reward for honest toil.

Do they, recipients of grace,
Ascend to some celestial place,
Enjoying as a well-earned plus
Eternal bliss along with us?

I rather hope, if truth be known,
They have a Heaven of their own.

# OUR DREAM HOUSE

When we build a new house, if ever we do,
We'll show that we've learned a thing or two:
A living room we shall do away with,
Since our family room is the one we stay with;
A dining room we can do without,
Since we eat in the kitchen or else dine out;
The closets and storage spaces and such
Will be larger, I'd say, than the rooms are, much;
The roof will be pitched (and with pitch) and won't
    leak,
While the doors won't stick and the floors won't
    squeak.
The yard will be lawnless and very small—
Mostly rocks, and no need for a mower at all. . . .
My intentions are good, I'm no stupid or bad man,
But the architect surely will think me a madman.

# FINDERS KEEPERS

Many young drop-outs say they are trying to "find themselves."—*News item*


The drop-out drops from school and home
And goes to Paris or to Rome
Or anywhere, since home's a bore,
Say with the family next door.

The drop-out who's not effervescing
Is somewhat droopy, adolescing;
And, turning inward, introspects
And is preoccupied with sex.

The search is on, in psychic shelves,
As drop-outs try to find themselves.
"Who," they ask themselves, "am I?"
And sometimes "Where?" and sometimes "Why?"

Someday the drop-out, sure as sin,
For no good reason will drop in,
And please don't ask, so he can hear,
"And did you find yourself, my dear?"

It's quite enough the lost is found
And good again to have around.

# HIGH POINT OF THE YEAR

Why the smile? Why the look of vigor?
Why the springing along on my toes?
Why the chest out and breathing deeply
Through dilated, upturned nose?

Only hours ago I was gloomy,
In fact on the edge of a tear.
My cheeks had a chalky pallor
That *could* have been caused by fear.

But now there's a change that's fantastic,
And it all came about in this way:
I've come from my annual checkup
And my doctor has said I'm O.K.

## FUTURE TENSE

I don't possess a crystal ball,
The future I can't see at all,
But still I have no slightest doubt
Of how, one day, things will come out.
I forecast, I prognosticate.
There is no need for you to wait;
Just ask me, and you'll get the lowdown
On economic upswing, slowdown,
On war and peace, on whatsoever,
A year from now, ten years, whenever.
This I have learned, each passing day:
The less I know, the more I say.

# WELL, COME IN

You can have your Welcome mats.
I ask for just a little more
When I come home from work, and that's
A Welcome mate inside my door.

# ABOUT THE AUTHOR

**Richard Armour** has led a double life as a professor and scholar and as a popular writer of humor and satire. A Harvard Ph.D., he has taught at a number of colleges and universities, has written books of biography and literary criticism, has held research fellowships in England and France, and has even been a dean of the faculty and a trustee. He has lectured or been guest-in-residence on more than 200 campuses in this country and has made five tours as a lecturer for the State Department in Europe and Asia.

But he is best known for his writing of light verse and prose for the leading magazines of the United States and England, and for his many books on a wide variety of subjects—books which have become classics of humor. His *Writing Light Verse and Prose Humor* is the standard work on the field in which he works—or plays.

As for his light verse, it began with his writing for *The New Yorker* and *The Saturday Evening Post* nearly forty years ago.

Richard Armour lives in Claremont, California, and spends most of his time observing and writing about the foibles of the human race and especially his own.

# ABOUT THE ILLUSTRATOR

**Henry Syverson** was born in Duluth, Minnesota, but is now, with his wife, a resident of Pine Bush, N.Y. He began his art career with the Walt Disney Studios, where he had a hand in creating such classics as *Pinocchio*, *Fantasia*, and the lovable antics of Pluto. He is much in the public eye these days, since his mad, scrambling characters appear regularly on *The Saturday Evening Post's* humor page, "Post Scripts," as well as in *Family Weekly*. He is a member of the Aircraft Owners and Pilots Association, which is perhaps why Pan Am sought him out when they wanted to turn their familiar but austere logo into something warmer and friendlier. These days it appears in many guises thanks to Mr. Syverson's whimsy—a balloon, a magic carpet, a pumpkin complete with white mice.